AARON RODGERS

SUPERSTAR QUARTERBACK

BY WILL GRAVES

Book design by Jake Nordby
Cover design by Jake Slavik

Photographs ©: Ryan Kang/AP Images, cover, 1; Rick Osentoski/AP Images, 4; Paul Sancya/ AP Images, 7; Detroit Lions/AP Images, 8–9; Shutterstock Images, 9; Paul Sakuma/AP Images, 10; Elaine Thompson/AP Images, 12; Darron Cummings/AP Images, 15; Julie Jacobson/ AP Images, 16; Morry Gash/AP Images, 18; Mark Humphrey/AP Images, 21; Scott Boehm/ AP Images, 22, 26; Matt Ludtke/AP Images, 25; Red Line Editorial, 29; David Stluka/ AP Images, 30

Press Box Books, an imprint of Press Room Editions.

Library of Congress Control Number: 2020901605

ISBN
978-1-63494-213-3 (library bound)
978-1-63494-231-7 (paperback)
978-1-63494-249-2 (epub)
978-1-63494-267-6 (hosted ebook)

Distributed by North Star Editions, Inc.
2297 Waters Drive
Mendota Heights, MN 55120
www.northstareditions.com

Printed in the United States of America
082020

About the Author

Will Graves has worked for more than two decades as a sports journalist and since 2011 has served as correspondent for The Associated Press in Pittsburgh, Pennsylvania, where he covers the NHL, the NFL, and Major League Baseball as well as various Olympic sports.

TABLE OF CONTENTS

1 HAIL RODGERS

The Green Bay Packers needed a miracle. It's a good thing they had a quarterback who knows a thing or two about making miracles happen.

It was December 3, 2015. Green Bay trailed the Detroit Lions by two points late in the fourth quarter. The Packers were in a tough spot. They had lost four of five games and needed a victory to give their playoff hopes a boost.

That's when Aaron Rodgers went to work. The veteran quarterback had long

Aaron Rodgers needed to make a play with his arm and his legs to beat the Lions in 2015.

been one of the most accurate passers in the National Football League (NFL). That night against the Lions, he needed both accuracy and a little luck. The Packers were 61 yards away from the end zone. And they had time for only one more play.

One play is all it took. Rodgers took the shotgun snap and scrambled to his left. The Lions quickly closed in, looking for a game-ending sack. Rodgers used some fancy footwork to escape. Then he sprinted to his right and unloaded.

The ball sailed high in the air on its way to the end zone. Players from both

REPEAT SUCCESS

Aaron Rodgers said the "Hail Mary" against the Lions was the first one he'd ever completed. He didn't have to wait long for his second. Rodgers struck again in the 2015 playoffs against Arizona. He connected with wide receiver Jeff Janis for a 41-yard Hail Mary on the last play of regulation. The touchdown tied the game, but the Packers lost in overtime.

Aaron Rodgers (top) celebrates with his teammates after their shocking comeback win.

teams leapt for it. Green Bay tight end Richard Rodgers, who is 6'4" tall, jumped higher than all of them. He hauled in the long pass in the end zone, giving the Packers a stunning 27–23 victory.

HAIL MARY

The Packers were trailing the Lions 23–21 with time for one more play. Quarterback Aaron Rodgers called for a Hail Mary pass. It worked, and Green Bay won the game.

HOW IT HAPPENED

1 The play starts at the Green Bay 39-yard line.

2 Rodgers takes the snap as four other Packers receivers run downfield.

3 Rodgers scrambles to his left, then circles back to his right, giving his receivers time to reach the end zone.

4 Rodgers heaves the ball high and long from his own 35-yard line. The ball travels 65 yards in the air to the Detroit end zone.

5 Richard Rodgers makes the catch to score the winning touchdown.

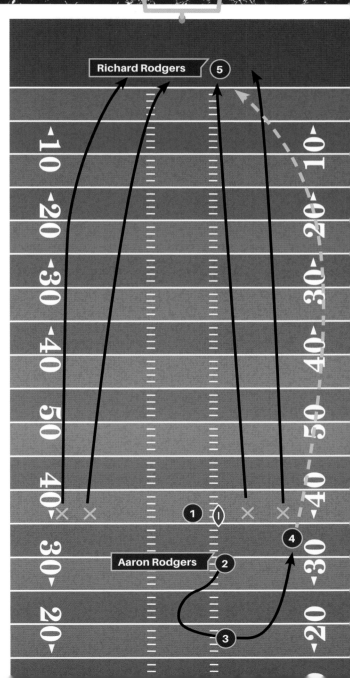

2 CALIFORNIA COOL

Aaron Rodgers discovered football when he was just two years old. He liked to sit in front of the TV in his parents' house in Chico, California, and watch NFL games for hours.

By the time he was five, Aaron could fire passes through a tire hanging from a tree. When he was in third grade, his right arm was so strong he could throw the ball over a neighbor's house. The ball would sail from the front yard to the backyard before splashing into the pool.

Aaron wasn't recruited heavily out of high school, but he eventually thrived at Cal.

Rodgers led Cal to a strong season in 2004.

Rodgers set a school record for passing yards during his senior year at Pleasant Valley High School. But most colleges thought he was too small to be a star quarterback. He thought about giving up football and concentrating on baseball. But he stuck with it, and it took him just one year at Butte Community College to prove himself. Rodgers led the Roadrunners to a 10-1 record in 2002. He passed for 2,408 yards and 28 touchdowns with just four interceptions.

The head coach at the University of California took notice. He offered Rodgers the chance to play for the Golden Bears in Berkeley, California. Rodgers wasn't sure he wanted to leave Butte. His coach at Butte joked he would drive Rodgers to Berkeley himself to make sure Rodgers played at the next level.

When he arrived in Berkeley, Rodgers was the

FROM THE HEART

Rodgers left college after his junior season in 2004, but the University of California—often referred to as "Cal"—remains close to his heart. In 2019 he donated a million dollars to the school. The money was used to renovate the locker room and fund the Aaron Rodgers Football Scholarship. The scholarship is awarded to a player who began his career at a junior college, just like Rodgers did.

backup quarterback at first. But he cracked the starting lineup in the fifth game of the 2003 season. By the next year, the player who was ignored coming out of high school was one of the best quarterbacks in the country.

Rodgers led the Golden Bears to a 10–2 record in 2004, with their only regular-season loss coming against national co-champion Southern California. He passed for 2,566 yards and 24 touchdowns. He finished ninth in voting for the Heisman Trophy, the award given every year to the best player in college football. Next stop? The NFL.

Rodgers put his athletic ability on display at the 2005 NFL Combine.

3 SLOW START, SUPER FINISH

Rodgers was ready to move on to the NFL in the spring of 2005. He attended the NFL Draft in New York City, expecting to be selected early.

The San Francisco 49ers had the top pick. Rodgers grew up rooting for the 49ers and wanted to join his favorite team. San Francisco chose another player instead. Rodgers had to wait hours for his name to be called. Finally, the Green Bay Packers chose Rodgers with the 24th pick.

A relieved Rodgers poses with his Packers jersey after being drafted late in the first round.

Rodgers spent three years on the bench as a backup to Hall of Famer Brett Favre.

The Packers already had a star quarterback in Brett Favre. When they picked Rodgers, they told him he had to wait to get a chance to play.

Rodgers sat on the bench for three years before Favre left in the spring of 2008. Rodgers knew it would be tough to replace a legend. His first season was rough. He passed for more than 4,000 yards, but the Packers finished with a losing record.

Rodgers led Green Bay to the playoffs in 2009. He threw for 30 touchdowns and was named to the Pro Bowl for the first time. He led Green Bay to the playoffs again in 2010, but the Packers were a long shot to reach the Super Bowl. They needed to win three road playoff games just

FROM RIVALS TO FRIENDS

Rodgers and Favre became friends after Favre left the Packers. When the two were teammates, they were not close. Favre did not like Rodgers at first because he knew Rodgers was going to one day replace him as the starting quarterback. The two patched things up after Favre retired. Favre even called Rodgers the best player in the NFL.

to get there. That was fine by Rodgers. He was used to following a long path to success.

Green Bay won playoff games at Philadelphia, Atlanta, and Chicago to reach the Super Bowl for the first time since 1996. The Pittsburgh Steelers and their top-ranked defense awaited in the big game. Rodgers picked the Steelers apart. He threw for 304 yards and three touchdowns as Green Bay beat Pittsburgh 31–25.

Rodgers was named the Super Bowl Most Valuable Player (MVP). The award completed his long journey from forgotten college recruit to NFL champion.

Rodgers hoists the Lombardi Trophy after winning the Super Bowl on February 6, 2011.

4 HEAD OF THE PACK

Some players relax after winning the Super Bowl. Rodgers used Green Bay's big win as the jumping-off point to becoming one of the NFL's all-time greats.

The year after helping the Packers win it all, Rodgers was even better. He was named the NFL's MVP in 2011 while leading Green Bay to a 15–1 record. Rodgers passed for 45 touchdowns and just six interceptions in 2011. His passer rating of 122.5 set an NFL record.

Rodgers put up incredible numbers on his way to winning the NFL MVP Award in 2011.

Rodgers was just getting started. The player who could throw a football through a tire at age five became one of the most accurate quarterbacks in NFL history.

He also proved to be one of the toughest. Rodgers won a second MVP award in 2014 when he passed for 38 touchdowns and five interceptions. He played the final two games of that season with a leg injury that made it difficult to walk. That did not stop him from running for a touchdown and throwing for two more in a win over Detroit that helped the Packers win the division title.

The only thing the Packers did not do during Rodgers' prime years is return to the Super Bowl. It was hard to blame Rodgers.

A hobbled Rodgers limped through a 2014 win over the Lions that put Green Bay in the playoffs.

Under first-year head coach Matt LaFleur, Rodgers led the Packers to a division title in 2019.

He thrilled Packer fans year in and year out with his clutch play.

In a playoff game against the Dallas Cowboys in January 2017, he made one of the best throws of his career. The game was tied with 12 seconds left. The Packers faced third down and 20 yards to go. They needed a big play. Rodgers drew one up in the huddle. He told each player where to run. Then he found tight end Jared Cook for a 36-yard gain. Green Bay won it with a field goal on the next play.

Though it looked like Rodgers made up the play on the spot, he had been thinking about it for months. It's just one of the many ways in which Rodgers was always two steps ahead of the competition.

STREAKING

Most quarterbacks feel they've done a pretty good job if they go an entire game without throwing an interception. Rodgers has gone months at a time without throwing the ball to the other team. Rodgers set an NFL record in 2018 when he threw 402 passes in a row without an interception. The opponents needed a little luck to finally get a pick on Rodgers. The pass that ended the record streak was tipped into the air, giving Chicago's Eddie Jackson time to run under and catch it.

TIMELINE

1. **Chico, California (December 2, 1983)**
   Aaron Rodgers is born.

2. **Oroville, California (2002)**
   Rodgers throws for 2,156 yards and 26 touchdowns for Butte College.

3. **Champaign, Illinois (September 20, 2003)**
   Rodgers makes his first start for the University of California, throwing for 263 yards and a touchdown in a 31–24 win over Illinois.

4. **New York, New York (April 23, 2005)**
   The Green Bay Packers take Rodgers with the 24th overall pick in the NFL Draft.

5. **Green Bay, Wisconsin (September 8, 2008)**
   In his first start for the Packers, Rodgers completes 18 of 22 passes for 178 yards and a touchdown in a win over Minnesota.

6. **Arlington, Texas (February 6, 2011)**
   Rodgers is named the Super Bowl MVP after throwing for 304 yards and three touchdowns against Pittsburgh.

7. **Phoenix, Arizona (January 31, 2015)**
   Rodgers receives his second NFL MVP Award in a ceremony before the Super Bowl.

8. **Minneapolis, Minnesota (December 23, 2019)**
   The Packers beat the Vikings to clinch the NFC North title.

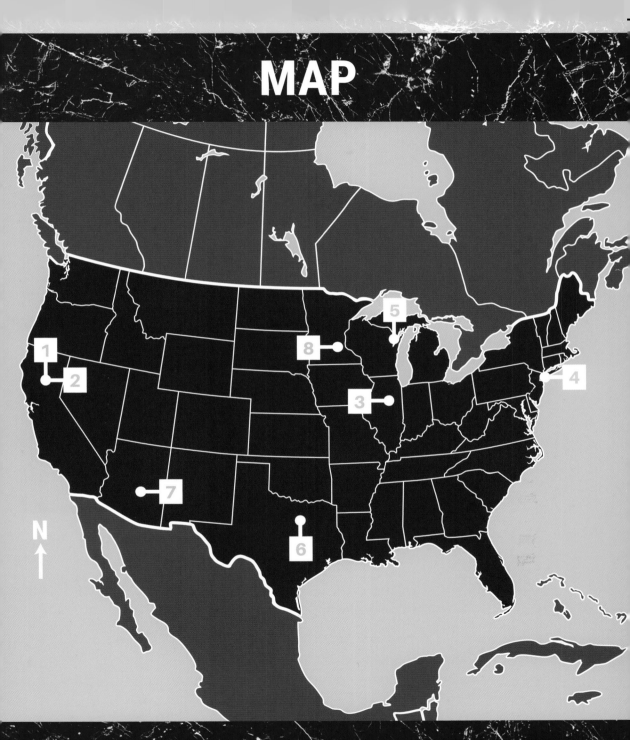

AT-A-GLANCE

Birth date:
December 2, 1983

Birthplace: Chico, California

Position: Quarterback

Throws: Right

Height: 6 feet 2 inches

Weight: 225 pounds

Current team: Green Bay Packers (2005–)

Past teams: California Golden Bears (2003–04)

Major awards: Super Bowl XLV MVP (2011), NFL MVP (2011, 2014), No. 1 among NFL Network Top 100 Players of 2012

Accurate through the 2019 NFL season and playoffs.

GLOSSARY

draft
A system that allows teams to acquire new players coming into a league.

Hail Mary
A long pass to the end zone at the end of a half or a game.

huddle
A gathering of players on offense and defense where they call plays.

interception
A pass intended for an offensive player that is caught by a defensive player.

passer rating
A formula that uses statistics to figure out how well a quarterback plays. A rating over 100 is considered excellent.

sack
A tackle of the quarterback behind the line of scrimmage before he can pass the ball.

scramble
To run around with the ball behind the line of scrimmage while looking for an open receiver.

shotgun
A formation in which the quarterback lines up 3 or 5 yards behind the center and takes the snap in the air.

TO LEARN MORE

Books

Myers, Dan. *Green Bay Packers*. Minneapolis, MN: Abdo Publishing, 2017.

Kortemeier, Todd. *Pro Football by the Numbers*. North Mankato, MN: Capstone Press, 2016.

Wilner, Barry. *Hard-to-Beat Sports Records*. Minneapolis, MN: Abdo Publishing, 2018.

Websites

Cal Bears Football
www.calbears.com/sports/football

Green Bay Packers
www.packers.com

NFL
www.nfl.com

INDEX